Modern Pirates

D1465976

NEL YOMTOV

Children's Press®
An Imprint of Scholastic Inc.

Content Consultant
Albert E. Scherr
JD, Chair
International Criminal Law and Justice Programs
University of New Hampshire School of Law
Concord, New Hampshire

Library of Congress Cataloging-in-Publication Data
Yomtov, Nelson.
 Modern pirates / Nel Yomtov.
   pages cm. — (A true book)
 Includes bibliographical references and index.
 ISBN 978-0-531-21466-4 (library binding) — ISBN 978-0-531-22079-5 (pbk.)
 1. Pirates—Juvenile literature. 2. Pirates—History—21st century. I. Title.
 G535.Y66 2016
 364.16'4—dc23   2015023741

Front cover: A Somali pirate stands near a captured Taiwanese vessel that has washed ashore

Back cover: A rescue team tows a lifeboat from the *Maersk Alabama* after the ship was hijacked by pirates

Find the Truth!

Everything you are about to read is true *except* for one of the sentences on this page.

Which one is **TRUE**?

T or F Modern pirates are more dangerous than pirates of the past.

T or F It is easy to capture today's pirates with high-tech equipment.

Find the answers in this book.

Contents

THE **BIG** TRUTH!

4

Pirate ships in the 17th and 18th centuries sometimes used special flags.

4 The War on Piracy

How do ships attempt to fight off pirate attacks?......................... **39**

According to official records, piracy off the coast of Somalia peaked in 2011.

5

Modern pirates across the world have access to powerful weapons.

CHAPTER 1

Danger on the Seas

On February 2, 2015, dozens of armed men boarded an oil **tanker** anchored off the coast of Nigeria in Africa. The men were pirates. They stole oil from the ship and took three crew members prisoner. One of the ship's officers was killed in the attack. The prisoners were later released, but the attackers were never caught. Even in the 21st century, pirates exist in large numbers. In fact, sea piracy is a major worldwide problem.

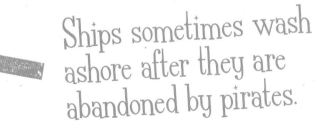

Ships sometimes wash ashore after they are abandoned by pirates.

What Is a Pirate?

A pirate is someone who commits robbery or any other act of violence for personal gain on the sea or ocean. Pirates are criminals, and many are vicious and murderous. Among their victims are ships' officers and crew members, people traveling on luxury vessels, and even ordinary fishermen. Although pirates are big news today, piracy is not new. It has been going on since people began traveling the seas thousands of years ago.

In parts of Nigeria, pirates sell containers of stolen fuel on the street.

Phoenician pirates prowled the waters around the Mediterranean Sea.

Ancient Pirates

The earliest documents about piracy describe the Lucca and Sherden peoples of the Mediterranean Sea. These pirates attacked boats off the coast of present-day Turkey in the 14th century BCE. About 2,000 years ago, Phoenician pirates of western Asia and northern Africa attacked ships. They took prisoners and sold them as slaves. Around the same time, pirates from Greece and Rome roamed the Mediterranean. Greek and Roman ports were frequent targets of their **raids**.

Viking raiders approach land.

The Middle Ages

From the late 8th into the 11th century CE, Vikings sailed from Denmark, Sweden, and Norway. They raided ships and coastal settlements in western Europe. The Vikings were excellent shipbuilders and highly skilled sailors. In time, their raids extended along North Africa, the Middle East, and central Asia. By the 13th century, the Wokou pirates of Japan began raiding ships in the Far East. They would continue their attacks for more than 300 years.

The Golden Age of Piracy

In the 15th century, European nations began establishing **colonies** in the Americas. Vast numbers of ships carried valuable agricultural products, gold, and other goods from the colonies to Europe. The Caribbean Sea was a main waterway, and it became a favorite hunting ground of pirates. This was particularly true between about 1650 and 1725. This era became known as the Golden Age of Piracy.

Spanish ships full of valuable cargo fill the waters around Cuba in the 17th century.

During this time, pirates from Great Britain, Spain, France, and other nations fearlessly attacked ships around the Caribbean islands. Blackbeard, Captain Kidd, and Henry Morgan are legendary examples. They raided vessels carrying slaves from Africa to the colonies, or carrying rum, sugar, and other goods to Europe. The most successful Golden Age pirate was Bartholomew Roberts, known as Black Bart. Born in Wales, Roberts captured more than 400 ships.

Black Bart's travels reached from West Africa to Brazil and all the way north to Newfoundland.

Women Pirates

Anne Bonny and Mary Read were women pirates during the Golden Age of Piracy. Anne and her husband, John "Calico Jack" Rackham, raided ships among the islands of the Caribbean. Mary Read fought alongside them. The team enjoyed much success. The colonial government in Jamaica captured all three in 1720 and **convicted** them of piracy. There is no official record of what happened to Anne. Mary died in prison of a violent fever. Calico Jack was hanged.

Barbary Pirates

Also in the 17th century, pirates from the Barbary Coast along northern Africa began terrorizing ships in the Mediterranean. Barbary pirates stole cargo and took crew members and passengers as slaves. Between the 16th and 19th centuries, the pirates captured and sold roughly 1 million people. In 1805 and 1815, the United States defeated the pirates and the governments that supported them in two wars known as the Barbary Wars. This helped halt piracy in the region.

Barbary pirates included many highly successful leaders, such as Turgut Reis.

Piracy in North America

From the late 18th to mid-19th century, pirates operated along the Ohio and Mississippi Rivers. They attacked river travelers and stole cargo, livestock, and slaves. Pirates also worked in the Great Lakes. There, they robbed victims of lumber, animal skins and meat, and even entire ships.

The goal of piracy has always been to steal. Modern pirates, however, are far more dangerous than pirates of the past. Their threat to society is also farther reaching.

Daniel "Roaring Dan" Seavey was perhaps Lake Michigan's most infamous pirate.

Modern pirates may steal valuable oil from an oil rig, or they may kidnap crew members.

The Face of Pirates Today

In some regions of the world, no type of boat is safe from pirate attack. Modern pirates target huge cargo and container ships, oil tankers, **yachts** and cruise ships, and even small fishing boats. Some pirates also attack offshore **oil rigs**, which drill for oil in the ocean. Attempted attacks on oil rigs have become more frequent in recent years, especially off the coast of western Africa.

 Offshore oil rigs are difficult to defend against pirate attacks.

Rescuers from the U.S. Navy help crew members on a fishing boat recently released by Somali pirates.

What Do Pirates Want?

Modern pirates are involved in several types of criminal activities. Some pirates attack and rob ships for cash, valuable equipment, and the crew's personal belongings. Others attack tankers and steal oil or chemicals. Some pirates hijack a ship and take the crew hostage. The pirates hold both the ship and the crew for ransom, which is a payment demanded for the ship and crew's return.

A Threat to Human Safety

The most serious impact of piracy is the threat to human life and safety. In recent years, pirates have taken hostage, injured, or killed thousands of people. In 2015, pirates from Somalia freed four Thai fishermen after holding them captive for nearly five years. Several other people who had been held hostage died before the release.

Egyptian fishermen sailing home wave to welcomers after escaping from pirates who had held them hostage.

A cargo ship refuels in open water.

The World Bank estimates that piracy costs industries and individuals about $18 billion a year.

The Economic Impact

Modern pirates also threaten international trade and the world's energy supply. About 90 percent of the world's food, raw materials, manufactured goods, and fuel are delivered by sea. To avoid pirates, shippers are forced to change their routes and use more fuel. A high risk of piracy also means shippers pay more for insurance in case they lose their cargo. This results in higher costs to consumers.

Waterborne Gangs

Many modern pirates use an assortment of weapons, such as automatic rifles and handguns. Some use high-powered grenade launchers and antitank missiles. A gang of pirates usually attacks a large ship in one or more small, fast motorboats. Sometimes they attack at night. To board a ship, pirate gangs may use ladders or grappling hooks and ropes. Once aboard, they take command of the ship. Then they begin the business of robbing or kidnapping the crew and passengers.

Pirates can hijack huge ships using just a few small motorboats.

Unsafe Waters

Pirates attack vessels in nearly all of the world's major waterways. Over the course of the 21st century, piracy has spread from West Africa's Gulf of Guinea and Somalia in eastern Africa to the coasts of India, Bangladesh, and Southeast Asia.

Most recently, roughly half of the world's attacks occurred around Indonesia and Malaysia. **Bulk carriers** and tankers were the most common targets, and nearly 450 **seafarers** were taken hostage there in 2014 alone.

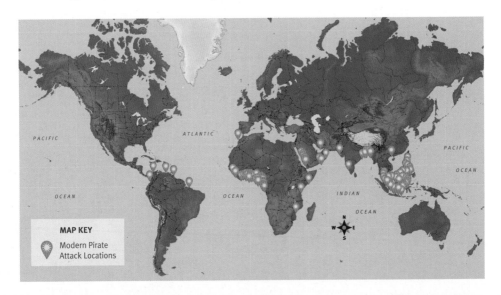

MAP KEY

Modern Pirate Attack Locations

A police officer in Kenya inspects weapons taken from possible pirates about to go on trial.

Big-Time Crime

Many pirate gangs have connections to large, well-organized criminal networks. These organizations' activities often include **trafficking** in human beings, illegal drugs, and weapons. The impact of these crimes can be devastating. The widespread availability of drugs and guns, for example, contributes to social and political unrest. This is especially true in poor countries. Some criminal networks aided by pirate activities may even be financing terrorist groups.

Severe poverty in places such as Indonesia makes piracy a tempting option.

Why Now?

Maritime piracy boomed in the 21st century. Money is one major reason. High unemployment motivates many poor young men to become pirates. In addition, a worldwide increase in sea traffic makes piracy easier. The willingness of shipowners to pay ransoms is another encouragement. Today's pirates also have easy access to high-tech communication devices, such as cell phones and Global Positioning Systems (GPS), and powerful weapons. They use these to track and attack their victims.

Public Acceptance

Piracy has cost many lives and billions of dollars in ransom and stolen cargo. But in some poor countries, piracy has brought economic development and growth. In areas in Somalia, for example, piracy provides livelihoods to merchants, fishermen, and other workers. Pirates spend the ransom money they receive in their communities, which supports their local economies. Pirates buy new homes, cars, electronics, and other items.

Piracy makes far more money for people than catching and selling fish, and it brings more money into the community.

The Parts of a Pirate Ship

While today's pirates often rely on small, speedy motorboats, seafaring thieves of the past sailed aboard huge wooden ships. These vessels were equipped with everything pirates needed to make long voyages and go head-to-head in battle with large cargo ships. A single ship might have held dozens of pirates.

1 RUDDER
Turning this piece of the ship from side to side helped control its direction.

2 GUNPORTS
These windows allowed pirates to fire on their targets while remaining protected below deck.

3 CANNONS
These powerful weapons launched huge balls of metal into enemy ships.

4 LIVING QUARTERS
Pirates did not have comfortable living areas. They often slept in cramped, dirty spaces, and rats were a common sight.

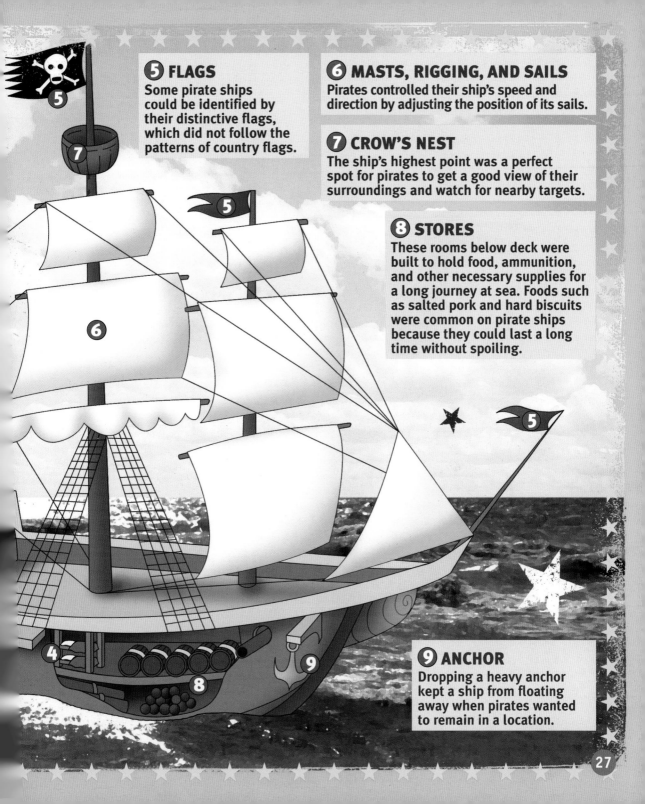

5 FLAGS
Some pirate ships could be identified by their distinctive flags, which did not follow the patterns of country flags.

6 MASTS, RIGGING, AND SAILS
Pirates controlled their ship's speed and direction by adjusting the position of its sails.

7 CROW'S NEST
The ship's highest point was a perfect spot for pirates to get a good view of their surroundings and watch for nearby targets.

8 STORES
These rooms below deck were built to hold food, ammunition, and other necessary supplies for a long journey at sea. Foods such as salted pork and hard biscuits were common on pirate ships because they could last a long time without spoiling.

9 ANCHOR
Dropping a heavy anchor kept a ship from floating away when pirates wanted to remain in a location.

From 2009 to 2011, Somali pirates attacked or attempted to attack 529 ships.

A pirate stares out at sea on the coast of Somalia.

CHAPTER 3

Hot Spots and Notable Pirate Attacks

Somalia lies on the Gulf of Aden, which links the Red Sea to the open Arabian Sea. These waters are important shipping lanes. Each year, tens of thousands of ships carrying oil, food, and other vital supplies pass along the Somali coast. This makes it the perfect spot for modern piracy to flourish.

Pirates prepare to board the *Faina* from their small boats in 2008.

The Hijacking of *Faina*

On September 25, 2008, Somali pirates captured the Ukrainian-operated carrier *Faina*. The ship was headed to Kenya with tanks and other weapons. The pirates took the *Faina* and its crew to the Somali port of Hobyo. They demanded money and threatened to kill the crew if they were not paid. One hostage had died by February 2009, when a Ukrainian businessman gave the pirates a $3.2 million ransom. The *Faina* and its surviving crew were released.

The *Sirius Star*

Somali pirates also made headlines in November 2008 after hijacking the oil tanker *Sirius Star* off the coast of Kenya. The ship had a cargo of oil worth $100 million. The pirates sailed the ship and its crew to Somalia and demanded a $25 million ransom. They released the ship the following January after receiving about $3 million. The *Sirius Star* crew was unharmed, but five pirates drowned when their smaller boat sank in a storm after leaving the ship.

Pirates held *Sirius Star* off the coast of Harardhere, Somalia, until they were paid ransom.

The *Maersk Alabama*

The most famous pirate attack off Somalia occurred on April 8, 2009. Four armed Somali pirates attacked and seized the American-registered cargo ship *Maersk Alabama*. The crew of *Maersk Alabama* regained control of the ship and captured one of the pirates. The three remaining pirates took the ship's captain, Richard Phillips, and left the *Maersk Alabama* in a lifeboat. They held him hostage, hoping to receive a large ransom.

The story of the Maersk Alabama hijacking was made into the film Captain Phillips.

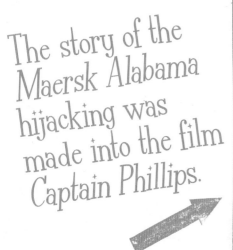

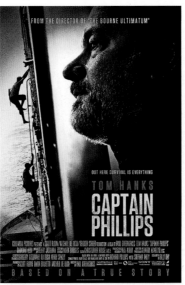

Actor Tom Hanks played *Maersk Alabama* captain Richard Phillips in the film about the ship's 2009 hijacking.

Maersk Alabama captain Richard Phillips (right) shakes hands with one of his rescuers, Commander Frank Castellano of the U.S. Navy.

Meanwhile, U.S. warships followed the lifeboat as it headed toward Somalia. During the next two days, navy officials tried to **negotiate** with the pirates to free Phillips, but they failed. On April 12, it seemed the captain's life was in danger. U.S. Navy SEAL **snipers** aboard a warship shot and killed the three pirates on the lifeboat. Captain Phillips was rescued unharmed.

Over the years, more companies began placing armed guards on ships and international navies increased their patrols in the waters around Somalia. This has helped cut down on piracy in the area.

Piracy on Falcon Lake

Thousands of miles away, Mexican pirates attacked American fishers on Falcon Lake. This lake lies on the border between the United States and Mexico. In a series of raids in 2010, members of a drug ring boarded American fishing boats and stole cash. The pirates used small fleets of speedboats to attack the fishing boats and to smuggle drugs into the United States. U.S. National Guard troops were sent to the area to prevent further attacks.

The U.S. Coast Guard patrols Falcon Lake, keeping an eye out for possible pirates.

U. S. COA G AR

Indonesia: The Newest Hot Spot

Since 2012, the largest pirate attack zone has shifted to western Indonesia. The region is an excellent target for pirates. One-third of the world's shipping moves through the Straits of Malacca and Singapore there. Pirates in and around Indonesia mainly steal cargoes of oil. They sell the oil illegally, often to large refineries.

The Lost Tanker

In May 2014, armed pirates hijacked the oil tanker MT *Orapin 4* in the Strait of Malacca. The pirates locked up the *Orapin*'s crew and destroyed the ship's communications equipment. Then they drained the tanker's cargo of 980,000 gallons (3.7 million liters) of fuel into another ship and fled. What became of the *Orapin*? Officials wondered. Four days after the attack, the ship arrived safely in a Thailand port. No one had been harmed, but there was no oil on board.

After being attacked by pirates, the crew of the *Orapin 4* was unable to contact officials until they reached port in Thailand.

Attacks on Yachts

Pirate attacks on yachts often go unreported, yet they occur throughout the world. Many attacks occur in Somali waters and the Gulf of Aden. In the Mediterranean Sea, armed robbers attacked the yacht *Tiara* off the island of Corsica in August 2008. The pirates stole jewelry, artwork, and $204,000 in cash. Off the coast of Brazil, pirates boarded the yacht *Maclow* in December 2008. The attackers stole cash, equipment, and personal belongings before escaping.

A member of the
U.S. Coast Guard
uses a Long Range
Acoustic Device.

CHAPTER 4

The War on Piracy

The shipping industry uses several nondeadly weapons to prevent pirate attacks. They include electric fences surrounding a ship that prevent pirates from climbing aboard. The Long Range Acoustic Device (LRAD) produces painful, high-pitched noises that drive away attackers. Water cannons shoot powerful blasts of water, knocking down pirates trying to board. Another weapon sprays a burning liquid called Mace on pirates. This forces them to jump back into the water.

The LRAD can also be used to send messages and warning tones over very long distances.

Technology at Work

The Possum is an antipiracy system that uses a series of "pods" placed around the outside of the ship. When pirates approach the ship, a crew member turns on the system. The pods shoot a cloud of burning chemicals. They also release nets that jam the propellers of the pirates' vessels. The Possum system has cameras and communication devices. This way, either the ship's crew or a team on land can operate it.

Timeline of Piracy

8th to 11th century CE

Vikings raid ships and towns in western Europe.

About 1650 to 1725

The Golden Age of Piracy flourishes in the Caribbean Sea.

Facing Limits

Even with these weapons, fighting piracy is difficult. The biggest challenge is preventing attacks and catching the attackers. International task forces and **coalitions** such as CTF-151 (Combined Task Force 151) and ReCAAP (Regional Cooperation Agreement on Combating Piracy and Armed Robbery Against Ships in Asia) help police the waters. The oceans are huge, however, and patrols cannot be everywhere at once. In addition, piracy changes locations. As incidents decrease in one place, they increase in another.

Early 1800s
The United States defeats pirates along the coast of northern Africa in the Barbary Wars.

April 8, 2009
Somali pirates hijack the cargo ship *Maersk Alabama*.

2012
The straits around Indonesia become the world's most pirated waters.

41

Four men were arrested for piracy in Nigeria.

Once pirates are arrested, there is another issue. Where should they be **prosecuted**, or put on trial? In the pirates' home countries? In the crews' home countries? There is no clear answer, and decisions may vary on a case-by-case basis. In such places as Somalia, piracy is a major source of income, and communities want it to continue. Also, governments in these states are often too weak to enforce the laws. In addition, piracy trials can be very expensive and the countries cannot afford them.

Kenya, Mauritius, and other nations that control the waters where attacks take place have put pirates on trial. Sometimes, countries cannot afford the necessary trials and prisons. For the *Maersk Alabama* and other American ships, U.S. courts have taken over. This has worked for American ships but does not necessarily apply to other nations' ships.

Countries around the world still search for the best way to fight piracy. This continued international effort provides hope for the years ahead. ★

Members of the U.S. military approach a boat they suspect was hijacked by pirates.

True Statistics

Number of reported actual and attempted pirate attacks worldwide, 2010–2014: 1,690

Cost of fighting piracy around Somalia in 2013 (including military operations, security, and labor): $3 billion to $3.2 billion, paid by governments and companies internationally

Largest ransom paid to Somali pirates: $13.5 million for the Greek-owned oil tanker *Irene SL* in 2011

Number of seafarers attacked by West African pirates in 2013: 1,871

Jail term for Abdiwali Muse, the surviving pirate of the *Maersk Alabama* hijacking: 33 years, 9 months

Did you find the truth?

(T) Modern pirates are more dangerous than pirates of the past.

(F) It is easy to capture today's pirates with high-tech equipment.

Resources

Books

Berlatsky, Noah, ed. *Piracy on the High Seas*. Detroit: Greenhaven Press, 2010.

Gilkerson, William. *A Thousand Years of Pirates*. Plattsburgh, New York: Tundra Books, 2009.

Malam, John. *You Wouldn't Want to Be a Pirate's Prisoner!* New York: Franklin Watts, 2013.

Peppas, Lynn. *Piracy*. New York: Crabtree Publishing Company, 2013.

Visit this Scholastic Web site for more information on modern pirates:

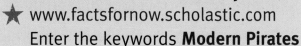 www.factsfornow.scholastic.com
Enter the keywords **Modern Pirates**

Important Words

bulk carriers (BULK KAR-ee-urz) — ships that carry dry, unpackaged cargo

coalitions (koh-uh-LISH-uhnz) —groups formed for a common purpose

colonies (KAH-luh-neez) — territories that have been settled by people from another country and are controlled by that country

convicted (kuhn-VIKT-id) — declared guilty of a crime

negotiate (ni-GOH-shee-ate) — to try to reach an agreement by discussing something or making a bargain

oil rigs (OYL RIGZ) — large platforms built above the sea as bases for drilling for oil under the ocean floor

prosecuted (PRAH-si-kyoot-id) — carried out legal action in a court of law against a person accused of a crime

raids (RAYDZ) — sudden, surprise attacks on a place

seafarers (SEE-fair-uhrz) —travelers who go by sea

snipers (SNIPE-urz) — people who shoot from a hidden place

tanker (TANG-kur) — a ship that contains large tanks for carrying liquids such as gas or oil

trafficking (TRAF-ik-ing) — buying and selling illegal goods

yachts (YAHTZ) — large boats or small ships with sails, used for pleasure or for racing

Index

Page numbers in **bold** indicate illustrations.

About the Author

Nel Yomtov is an award-winning author with a passion for writing nonfiction books for young readers. He has written books and graphic novels about history, geography, science, and other subjects.

Nel has worked at Marvel Comics, where he edited, wrote, and colored hundreds of titles. He has also served as editorial director of a children's book publisher and as publisher of Hammond World Atlas books.

Yomtov lives in the New York City area with his wife, Nancy, a teacher. Their son, Jess, is a sports journalist.